BIRD and TREE / IN PLACE

BIRD and TREE / IN PLACE, Poems , Peter Weltner © *2020*

Marrowstone Press
© *2020*
All rights reserved

ISBN: 978-0-578-71859-0

BIRD and TREE / IN PLACE

Poems

PETER WELTNER

That longing pausing wishing that cannot pass
Uncomprehended things without a sigh
For wisdom to unseal the hidden cause–
That 'ankering gaze is thine that fainly would
Turn the blue blinders of the heavens aside
To see what gods are doing.

John Clare, "A Ramble"

Book One
Bird and Tree

To the Memory of

Linda Gregg
Bill Mayer
Corbett Rouse
Bob Stephens
and for
Jason Wirth
Nathan Wirth

Table of Contents

I.

II.

I

Statements

1.

A romantic poet,
son of the last century
or long before, set
apart by what obsesses me,
a tragic sense of life, I find
in every
poem I write I am bidding goodbye
to something or someone, as if free
late in life to write
for the dead more than the living. Mourning
feels like a torchlight
I am carrying, borne
down to darkness by love. I am cold. It is snowing.
I cross the bridge into woods. I know where I have to go.

2.

He stands in the shade of a cactus grove in Joshua Tree,
the sun at its daily
work of searing
the desert to a blistering white, like nothing,
like the world vanishing at the end of days,
an illusion that stays
in the mind stricter than truth. There's an art
to luminosity
that is part
of its darkness,
the last bright glimpse of all one might see
at the moment of dying,
clear as a deathbed confession
of a life less lived than imaginary.

Poetry Is a Kind of Dying

I dreamed last night of a lake that lies
not far from the sea,
a bonfire
on its shore, its flames
sparking heavenward. By what names
do its people call this place? The sky's
cerulean blue, shadowy
over water on a cloudy day. Why
does it matter if desire
troubles an old man's body
with its inner fire,
sleeping while sleepless,
dreaming while awake, every yesterday
rewritten by tomorrow into the fool I now play?

So I floated in a boat on the beautiful blue lake,
discovering a cove where a lover
from years before, for my sake
I suppose, rose out of the water–
naked, blond, muscular–
soaring like an angel, hovering
in the sky,
who sang to me of death,
of pulse
and breath
and departure, nothing else
save seas,
poetry
spared by syllable and measure.

Les Chemins de Mélancolie

Remember the road we took, les entre-deux-guerres,
to the chateau of the Princesse, the American
sewing machine heiress, where
an haute-contre tenor whose voice began
flute-sweet then grew melancholy as an oboe
sang melodies, chansons, arias like moonlight on taut silk,
like the wisps of mist floating past a half curtained window
that opened toward hills shadowing a valley, milkwhite
ice floating on the fountains' pools, drifting downstream
toward the river. You gloried in an old silver spoon laid on an ancient gold
plate a venerable waiter offered us macarons on, like a dream
of an ancien regime, the carpet beneath our feet cold
as a grave, I complained as one too young to know, as he told
of hearing Clément singing Faust while he served his rarest wine to a thirsty Gounod.

Listening to Brahms on a Rainy Afternoon in Late Fall

A light drizzle skitters and skips across an olive bay,
holly, sorrel, fennel, crab grass a fading green, pale
as the mist sifting through trees. My love's far away.
I smell coffee beans roasting in a café. A horned snail
lies on the sidewalk, crushed by a shoe, its shell
broken amber flecks scattered over muddy ground.
A pink worm flails in a gritty puddle. I would do well
to think less of myself, love the world more. Nearby,
a bus clatters past its stop. An ambulance's sirens sound
like fear inside me. I stand on my deck. Insert the key. Try
not to listen to my wayward heart beat. Press the door
open. Enter a vacant bedroom. Play some treasured CDs.
How do we bear the cessation of life? Bad weather would be poorer
without Brahms. His scores' formal rooms. The lamp-lit solace of his melodies.

Water Music

You have traveled to a faraway land, my brother,
without father or mother, to a peace that could
not have been otherwise so many decades after
we had parted. Perhaps everything is fated, good
luck or bad. Even loneliness. Even solitude. A flock
of birds frightened by a snake rises through canopy
to an opening sky. We came to a crossroads. Shocking
us both, you pursued your way, I found mine. Every
pain has its reasons, you said. We somehow grew
old apart. Jonquils brighter than summer, a creek, red clay
in the days I first knew you, memories keen, if few:
the sun fading to twilight, cardinals mating, a jay
squabbling with a chipmunk, and the lake where we lay
all we would need to say about our lives, of how little we knew.

Bird and Tree

An agèd monk meditates on a hill
in a hut overlooking a gorge,
his mind quiet, thoughts still
as the oars he planted, the barge

he beached on a bank of a river
that flows over large rocks
battered by roiling white water.
A winter-cold wind shocks

him. In a dream-like after-
life, he sips rice wine,
hears children's laughter,
sees a secluded garden fine

as the emperor's in an old
ghost story of a drunken moon,
a white crane, a boat poled
by a stranger, and a jeweled loon

made of gold stolen from court
that flew into a mulberry
tree a few measures shorter
than the tallest Buddha. See

how I worship you, Lord, the monk
says to the bird that waits
for him by the cypress, each trunk
foreboding as a palace's gates.

As he wakes, the river overflows, brim-
ming with speckled carp. A water-
fall roars down cliffs, sprays him
with mist, splashes his face. The shiver

he feels comes from breezes, light
as the March air he breathes. He drinks
strong wine for warmth. It is right
to partake from life's cup, he thinks,

while lighting small logs for a fire,
from the wood left in the bin.
Which ought he desire
to be? A bird? Or the tree it nests in?

2.

Watch a star from the far east
bright as a bird of paradise
journey west like a beast
fearsome for the fire in its eyes.

Observe this golden star as it looms
over a mythic Palestine,
shines on a child it dooms
with its light, though not by design,

the new born in a manger
adored by shepherds, magi,
mother, yet in serious danger
from Herod's terror and envy.

Ass, ox, sheep, cows worship
him, too, incarnate word
in a day old baby, by whip
and sword soon to be exiled. Absurd,

one might say, the whole scenario.
But, notice, the star is no
star but a holy bird shed-
ing light on a child's wooden bed.

And the child understands, wis-
er than anyone guesses, knows
exactly what awaits him: to rise
from dead and so, reborn, disclose

the death of death. Let us suppose
his real mother is not Mary,
no, but the bird, the spirit that shows
the boy how to fly, not Joseph but the tree

his rooted, gnarled father. Which should
he choose to be, bird or the tree
it perches on, weighty wood
or a feathered thing? Tragedy

is like that, not just pain and loss
but a lover's embrace. Look above
the altar at the icon, the son a dove
with red wings splayed on a white pine cross.

Boy Puppeteer

I cannot ignore I am old,
though it feels like a trap,
like dying sooner
than I ought to. I'm told
I must accept it, its slap
of shame across my face making me wince from humiliation.

Long ago, in early June,
as I tanned on a beach
or swam with friends,
long past afternoon,
two lifeguards began a search
for a boy not drowned, but sneakily hiding in bushes. It all depends.

Back then, I played with puppets,
made them dance to visible
strings my fingers manipulated.
Imagination lets
a child hope anything is possible,
even raising a marionette or make-believe friend from the dead.

Sooner or later, I know I must stop
pretending I did dare
to do what I couldn't, swinging his door quietly
open, sneaking in barefooted drop-
a-pin silent to the bed where
Bob Murphy lay mimicking sleep while, terrified, I stroked his naked body.

Seventeen

A boy hunts for unbroken conch shells
as his dog scampers over a dune
where a man strips off his trunks. What tells
him so young love comes too soon
or too late? A swimsuit's waistband
snapping, a towel
drying hair, footsteps on sand,
the boy's dog growling
at him as the man kicks on
his flip-flops, bends to reach
for his blanket, walks away, gone
from the beach,
from his life, what might have begun
if the sea had not seethed that day from the heat of an afternoon sun.

A boy not knowing what to do, where to go,
wondering if they might have met
in a former life, gotten to know
each other, never to forget
their chance encounter. He sits on a bench,
listens. Come home with me.
His fingers clench,
clutching empty air. The man touches his knee.
Not to submit
but to regret he had not done it
while he absentmindedly
counts his shells, the sensuous whorls–
pink pearl and triton yellow and whelk white of the sea–
even as the sun spirals faster than a pinwheel and spins and swirls.

Boy Scout

Backyard woods, high grass, sumac, milkweed
to stalk through, to play soldiers,
erect pup tents in, a comic book to read
by an oil lamp when the weather's
foul, sleeping bag pitched on pine-needle-prickly
packed red clay, black beetles lumbering
over rocks, dusky moss, felt-soft on bark musty
as a trunk in an attic packed with nothing
but grandparents' clothes, and, on one November day,
a dead wren its feathers half-buried in gray
mud beside the creek, ants, white grubs, foot-long
red worms massing on it, a spider web knit among
dew-wet ferns, meshed tendrils thick as fat fingers,
and stones to throw at its bones to see how far it scatters.

Mentor

A forest creek rippling, leaves rustling in chilling
breezes. Cowbells past twilight. The spell
of night creatures rustling, insects' buzzing,
the moon's silvery gleaming, tiger moths swell-
ing en masse flapping their wings, starlight
seeping through oak, poplar, maple, sycamore,
pallid leaves frosted like grass in winter. A night
meant for us sick ones, you remarked before
you saw my stick poking at the carcass of a beaver,
its pelt spotted gray as mold. You begged me never
to forget you. "My writing is all the life I've known,"
you said. "It was never fame I so long labored after."
I saw you early this morning, a snake slithering toward water.
"How old you've grown," you said slinking away, "how sad and bitter you've grown."

Paradigms

Night, the stars off course, the sun, as at story time,
blackening. Five-toed frogs.
Salamanders big as hogs.
Bleeding rocks. Two headed dogs. A paradigm
of sorts. Grotesqueries. Residues
of deformed thoughts. A pine tree cracking apart,
smoldering, split by lightning.   I am losing
you again. Call it my broken heart,
why can't I? Clouds, mist blowing like veils on
the horizon
seen through a shadowy light and I left behind
deep into sorrow.   What shall I find
when I search for our last days together?
Promises. Words. "I will always be your friend. Your lover."

Ramrod

Maddened, enraged by the tyrannies of unreason,
dreading the thunder
rumbling in eastern clouds, the unseasonable
heat that makes his thoughts wander,

the sun white as snow
on mountains,
as the glow on Dionysos' face,
teeth-men's swords clashing on Theban plains,

awestruck, he contemplates a passion too bright
for logic, an ashen fire
like anthracite
smoldering in his brain, voices mimicking a women's choir,

men's songs exulting, laughing, at the ruin of a boastful
boy who won't let them fuck
him or risk getting lost
in ecstasy, subdued by a force more fateful than bad luck

while he hides in shadows, in his last moments watching a horror
show out of his need
to see what might happen if he should cross over
into the bar's backroom, giving in to transgressions, gorging on men's seed.

Stefan, Ten Years Old

A desert, airless as the moon, no wind.
A goat with a blood red rag
wrapped round its horns, a shaggy coat. How has it sinned,
its spine, whole body sagging
from mankind's evils?   A white salt plain
by the Dead Sea,
the mountains behind purplish, a bruise-like stain
to the haze. A lost goat, driven from the herd, bewildered and solitary.

Stefan mocked for his stutter, glasses, stumbling gait,
the stench of onions, coal on his clothes,
beaten with sticks, rocks wherever he goes.
Stefan, who cannot wait until he dies.
who, no matter how hard he tries,
will never be loved, exiled into his childhood, faultless and desolate.

Christmas Morning

Last night's storm passed through moments
too early. Bold, golden, a sliver of a moon
dips lower in the sky. Scents
of wet leaves and washed pavement. Soon,
full morning will arrive. Lights flickering, a jet
flies westward toward clouds breaking,
billowing like sails. My dog has set
his path on the ice plants. A shallow lake
the rain made is slick as sleet on the beach
with a deep green-blue marine-like sheen,
the waves shiny as a satin sash, rosy
white with a touch of yellow. I should reach
into my past this morning. I should ask it what it might mean
by failure, a gull's plaintive cawing as it challenges the sea.

Let Troy Live

Early morning dark is late night's promise for a better tomorrow.
Delayed for weeks by bad weather, crab boats' lights flame
like torches far out at sea. Old age is what you borrow
from time and must pay back the same
as any loan. The sea is rough, breaks
into zigzag patterns as waves crash past each other.
On the beach, a few surfers calculate the stakes,
ponder the risks of paddling out just before dawn, the danger
of unseen riptides. A semi passes me on the highway,
its wheels splashing water on the cars behind it
as if midnight's rains were still falling. Morning mist like bay
fog swells over coastal hills. When is it right to quit
believing in life, to say it is no longer worth
the effort, the hurt felt each dawn upon wakening of remaining on earth?

My body shocks me with new, inexplicable pains every day.
Friends die or are dying. Old age is a sort of war. The globe
is collapsing in disarray, too, into chaos from dismay
at men's acts against it. Yet dawn comes, like Joseph, in a robe
of many colors. Why does its splendor still surprise
us, the sun like a boy's golden hair tossed in a breeze
as it starts to rise. I think of the light cast off shields and greaves
and swords when the invaders woke up outside Troy's walls
and prepared for another day of killing, of tragedy and carnage,
warriors struck, stunned by a recognition of a possibility that appalls
them, makes them plea or pray to the gods they should rail and rage
against: that in this morning's bitter beauty they might find release
from their fates, sea lanes opening to return them home to a long, inglorious peace.

Hidden Lives

1.

The boy's hair glitters with sawdust, forearms
tapered like a baseball bat. He leans on
a broken, overgrown ladder. What harms
life comes to he knows well already, vines

and wild roses like snakes twined round its rungs.
The sun glares in his eyes as he poses
for a photo his mother takes. His lungs
feel clogged from the smoke of a neighbor's

fire as he burns wet hay. The boy's eyes are black
and suspicious as a hawk's. A rip in
his jeans shows a hole in his drawers, slackly
washed shirt brown and wrinkled as a paper bag.

Tobacco dust clogs his nostrils. The air tastes
like tin, cotton shriveled into weedy stalks.
Hail has trampled on the hay. A cow wastes
away, hens have quit laying, his ribs protrude like posts.

2.

Live indeed shall your dead for your dew
is the dew of light and the land of Sharon
shall give birth. Preacher bows his head to
the coffin, digs his fingers into earth, crumbles it,

scatters it like seeds. A sudden wind
topples his bowler hat off his head
and tosses it into the grave. That boy must've sinned,
preacher says to his father shoveling dirt in quick,

a hundred times faster than it took him to dig
it. Back home, the old man removes his son's gun
from its hook and tries it out for size, the trigger
fitting his finger better than it had his sickling boy's.

3.

The dead boy's brother's ears ache. His vomit is cow-cud
green. He hides in a closet, but when their father
sticks the hog its squeal pricks his eardrums sud-
den and loud as thunder. His slaughtering done, their father

showers off blood and stench. The boy sneaks away to try
on his brother's drawers. He wears them round
his neck like a cowboy's bandanna or, why
not, he thinks, on his head like an army cap. He loves

their old man, too, but his slap makes his head
dizzy as happens when he has been playing
crack-the-whip. His brother is dead, the bed
unmade where the boy sleeps, grieving alone his way.

4.

God's sky bound creatures. Doves, titmice, quail,
orioles, blackbirds. A soft squirrel-lined cloak,
his mother's, that he tries on, his face pale
as flour in her hand mirror. He pats on some rouge.

Outside, he shouts to scare the birds that soar
toward heaven, twirling faster and faster
into smaller and smaller rings. He isn't, no more,
who everyone thinks he is but a bird shining,

sun-bright as its swift flight blinds the sight
of each believer trying to see where
it might have flown to, like his brother reuniting
with the Lord in the light of His pitiless love.

5.

His faith in God forsaken, belief denied
him—creation in need of redemption, his suffering
suffered in the agony of Christ crucified,
what his father has testified, his mother has cried to—

he's a boy who feels unreal, woven from cotton or woolen
clothes, carved from hard wood or soft,
chiseled from stone or marble, turned to clay, then
re-moulded into the life he hides in where no one can find

him. His brother's light as dove's feathers where he lives
now, his mother says as she knits him a sweater
warm enough to defy fiercest winters, the gift she gives
to him repeating words he has heard often before,

"There's no need ever to fear the meanest cold, Son,
wearing so loving a sweater. The Lord will never
fail you, ask of you more than you can bear. Upon
my soul, I swear it": as she swore twice over to his wailing brother.

6.

Waterfall and snow-fed river and sheer mountain
peak they never climbed together, when
will he meet him there, his brother come again
to greet him, as angels do descending from heaven,

bringing news, or gossip, like villagers from the valley town,
survivors all, men women and children,
telling how the days have passed, how the brown
drought times have vanished, the waste of life finally over,

how death is nothing more than more than nothing
in the end, like the high-peaked mountains looming
over their farms, infinite, yet often disappearing
in foul weather until returning as Jesus vowed he would.

II

Sauratown

It is a muggy morning, shortly after first light,
mist obscuring Pilot Mountain
in the distance, a slight
breeze promising rain.
In a creek, fishermen
catch tadpoles in nets for bait,
the river in the valley teeming
with pike and bass best caught early. A pink gray, yellow white
light adorns the sky. Let full day wait
a while longer. Let noon be delayed. Let dawn gleam
resplendent forever. An old man looks,
grimacing, at his wrinkled, spotted, arthritic hands,
shaking his head as he dips his net, crooks
his fingers, the writhing fish he has caught the little he understands.

Migration

Migrating pelicans, a few geese,
plovers, white and gray
gulls feed at the shoreline
on fish the tide's brought in.

The sea's calm after days of rough
currents and high waves. Sleekly
feathered, bold geese swim
as if drifting in a park pond.

Pelicans circle above, their long,
wide wings flapping, then glide
in the breeze, their thin beaks
curved, sharp as scissors blades.

More birds rest as if patiently
waiting or carved from wood.
After they feast, they'll take
a last leave, fly away far off.

They are staring out to sea.
as if observing a rite,
in prayer perhaps, offering thanks
for the gift of good weather.

Walking their dogs off leash,
people let pets run free,
playing, barking, chasing,
pursuing what they can't catch.

Like one, the birds soar off in
the roar of a gust of wind
or a sudden storm, headed
northward to a place they'll mate in.

Like a dream of life, they fade
into sky and vanish. Standing
beside me you say just this:
We're either too young or too old to die.

Miracle

He enjoys watching his men
fish, savors the taste of their catch,
sweetly tender
on his tongue. Their wine
is pleasant to sip. He hears a snatch
of song, a riddling rhyme
that yields no answers, and talks
of the blessings ahead.
He has seen madmen who stare at the sun
meaning to go blind,
babbling about vision.
Death is already well behind
him or waiting nearby. He has said what he has said.
May you be whom he chooses, who picks up his mat and walks.

Uwharrie

After the storm's incessant rain, the sky is a slick slate gray,
the few marbled clouds not yet bled

dry. Birdsong, chattering squirrels, locust rasping the next day,
the river rising red

with Carolina clay, the rippling, churning water
breaking the sun into a thousand

rays silvery as fish scales. On the banks, bones' slivers glitter,
washed of mud and sand.

Posters on bridges warn of the river's flooding after storms without
warning. In nearby woods, you hear

hoarse breathing, a hard wind struggling to catch its breath, a shout
of desperation in the air,

a hesitation that questions your being there, dark clouds floating away
on the exhalations of dawn,

a light you cannot find a word for you try to articulate in the way
the river might after you and your friends are gone.

Snake

A tall boy roams in woods, picking
berry sprigs for luck as his father
would have done. When spring comes,
trees' canopies offer safest shelter

against sudden downpours lingering
after storms. Why does he fear
the snake slithering slowly from under
the slab he's poked with an oak limb?

He tosses rocks at it. It winds grace-
fully back to its lake. Snake, snake,
he shouts when it refuses to race
away, to obey its place in the world.

Pine resin bleeds from an aging tree's
bark, its needles intertwined with elm
and maple leaves. What if what he sees
were all there is, sunlight on a cloud

shining upon him as on an open
field too desolate to be fit for human
eyes and a snake, its poison the sin
men have misread from the beginning,

the moccasin slinking and gliding into
the lake, swimming, no omen, serpentine
sinuous, shimmering, beautiful
as fallen leaves floating in silvery water.

Late August

A bristling heat has rusted the leaves of gingko
trees. Geese flock to the lake in the park
for relief. A brown-feathered sparrow
chirps in a eucalyptus whose bark
peels like sunburnt skin. Insects
click, twitter, rasp, scrape, their white
noise like the voices science detects
when listening to outer space, like a rite
the cosmos chants in the manner
of Gyoto monks blessing a garden or praying
for peace in overtones that gather in a sound that collects
the subdued whispers of tired old people chattering
in a temple or at an altar, the murmur of late leaves rustling,
and a stream rushing through rocky cliffs near the end of a fertile summer.

A Cave in the Woods

Crushed, boneless, a squirrel's pelt
sprawls on an asphalt road melting into
the shoulders by kudzu and bamboo.
The man's leather belt
holds up his baggy, oversized blue
jeans. A stretch of dried clay
leads nowhere.
Past the underbrush and cane, the sun is disappearing
into the forest, night
descending in shadows dark as moss, stark
as trees and boulders. Like a kite
with a broken string, wide leaves twirl down. A dog is barking
far off, frightened
by wolves deeper in woods where they'll howl all night or bay.

The creek zigzags down slick red clay, its steep
bank thick
with rhododendron. The trick
is to grasp the vines and not slip deeper
into the ravine. Gnats swarm over a pool of trickling water
a skate darts on like a trapped fly.
The cave he sought is rank as the wet skinned fur
of a cat. He lights a match inside it. There's a rusty
red wound in the chest of something vaguely human lying
on the floor, a gap no bigger than a bullet hole,
a body stretched out, gun beside it, hidden from sight,
like someone quietly sleeping
where it is always night
telling of a deeper understanding of the trials of a soul.

Tomales Bay

Flowing slowly into the estuary,
the tide rustles reeds, cattails
growing from moss and boggy
ground at the end of a plank walkway.

The moonless sky sparkles gray-white, cloudy
with stars, winds
fiercer than any in the city,
trees and tall weeds crackling as they bend.

His is a monkish solitude among fir,
redwoods, live oak,
tides receding, shallow water
drifting back twice daily through the bay.

In the loneliness of late evening, he tries
to meditate, fails, eats
a supper of pocket pies
and cheese, washed down with beer.

All night, semis rolling down Sir Francis Drake
loaded with milk cans
and crates brake,
screeching, at the curve by his shack.

Early morning, in the eastern valley and hills,
pine, brush, scrub grasses
on sloping fields burn as dawn fills
the sky with a light like a forest in flames.

A century or more ago, a vast crack,
plates clashing northward,
left no way back
for the land to return to where

it began, like a world with no plan
to it, only a painful beauty,
like a life unmade by a man
who knows no better way to speak of pity.

Battle of Stones River

Shutters broken, shades drawn, peeling
paint curled like wood shavings,
the clapboard farmhouse is mourning
for him. He knocks. A tearful woman sings
in response, keens, kisses her son. With a long
spoon she points to a plank bridge.
What is wrong
in the view she shows him? A row of sedge
lines the creek, its cold water
deep from swells
of winter rains. It must be bedtime or just after,
the hour when the young go to sleep. He kneels
on a rock. The spring tastes bitter as quinine, salty
as the bloody river he drank his fill from last night in Tennessee.

Battle of the Wilderness

In the wilderness, the boy believes
only in carnage, dreads each coming battle, fears
dying more than death. His pleas
to Jesus proved fruitless as tears,
hurtful as thoughts of woods near his home, a cave
he'd hide in, the mountain behind their barn, the stream
he quenched his thirst in. Can you dig a grave
without a body to bury in it, redeem
its life somehow? He needs to stay awake,
must never sleep
again, be brave for his family's sake,
he and his men hunted like boars, trapped like sheep
in a pen. He hears his father chopping down a tree his brother
and he had swung on when young, still boys at the start of the slaughter.

Saratoga

In deepest winter cold, the moonlit field is brightened by snow
blanketing old gravestones hewn from upstate granite,
stark as boulder slabs as if each were yet to be chiseled

with name and dates of lives yet to be lived. Should I go
to the woods, the frozen river, the quarry pit,
roped off, blacker than night where I hear a lost dead

child crying in the ruins where a boy had drowned a decade
before the war? A grove of oak trees forms a silhouette
of men in great coats huddled snuggly arm in arm. I have read

how soldiers clashed on this field two centuries ago, were laid
to rest where they fell or were buried long after, commit-
ted to their God. I wish for earth's comfort, to sleep in my bed.

It is midnight, Christmas Eve. My family no longer waits. Yet I'm home.
I can see lights through the windows, smoke from the chimney.
They are reading my letters, repeating, telling each story more slowly.

What do they know? It is their memories that make me wander, roam
through haunted places. If you disbelieve in ghosts, reader, think of me.
Who walks as lost in this field beside me? Which of us weeps more bitterly?

Southern Baptists

Mating locusts rasping, louder than dry gourds rattling.
Steaming magnolia, verbena, thick humidity to bask in.
Like amber bits chipped from twilight, fireflies flickering.
Mown grass sweeter than hay, than fodder gathered in a bin.

Behind the church a cemetery,
its generations of names
and dates easy to see
daily scrubbed, flames
of geranium, salvia, poppies
licking each stone hewn
from neighboring mountains
by devoted members of their families.

Breathless men, women on a feverish June
night, trusting still in the Lord's swift return

Southern Gothic

Thunder in the clouds, the sky gazing at you with its sharp blue
eyes looking down on a field of flaming sunflowers.
Dreams should not require that you'll
believe upon wakening
what you knew to be true while sleeping, the cruelty
of vertiginous dark, the horror of no better world elsewhere.

Child, why do you cower before a wolf at the door,
at monsters that dare
to slip on snail-slick bellies
into the room you had carefully locked the night before?

Do you dread the world the more you dream of it? Heavy showers
wake you. A monster is shaking
your bed furious, enraged like Mary Shelley's
at having been created.   No more books, boy. No more shocking realities.

Widow

A great grief's hardest times must begin after
months of careful planning
for the memorial, announcements sent, laughter
and meals shared with friends trying
their best to help,
like the poets,
his friends, who believed they knew how he felt
when they wrote their elegies. Sorrow is truest when it lets
itself become the funeral,
the ceremonial
gathering, the poem
no one need read aloud. It is not the letting go,
the stoic show
of bearing up that speaks of your grief. It is his silence. Your empty home.

Southern Fundamentalism

The earth steams. Dark clouds rumble.
Cicada chirr, flies and bees buzz,
pond frogs croak, throb, grumble,
tree frogs whistle. The storm flees east.

A house of clay-colored weathered
bare planks. Tin roof. An open hall
leading through it, in one door, led
out the other. His mother darns and sews.

If they should hunger, the Lord takes
care. Tears turn to pearls some day.
As Jesus suffered for their sakes,
so must they suffer for those they love.

A cherry tree unlikely to ripen. A jug
for rain water with a hairline crack.
A pit for box turtles the boy dug
out of mud they'd drowned in one night.

Orioles, redwings, grackles, starlings,
jays. The snap of a twig, the crack
of a limb scares them away, Spring's
early. The water he drinks tastes good.

Their county is an impoverished place.
Some make do with what they grow.
To live in pain tests God's grace,
they say, tribulation tries their faith.

Poor means poorer than I am. His father
built their house. It needs repairing.
The roof tilts east, the gate's no better,
the porch dips south. Despair's the worst sin.

Butterfly bushes darken their windows.
Kudzu clings to clapboard like paint.
Man is measured by his shadows'
length. No boy like him could be a saint.

III

Politics (1)

The cameras' lights are out. The reporters have gone
to pursue other news. Except by a few,
the war will be forgotten soon, survivors abandoned, alone,
the dead ignored, no pictures, no names to attend to
or read on the front page, see on a screen,
the country returned to normal.
But black, flat spaces may be seen
to have redacted her thoughts. There's a wall
between those who know and those who don't. Her husband's
clothes hang in her closet. She tries
hard to rest but can't in their vacant bed. She understands
little but senses comforting words are the cruelest sort of lies.
She stares at a bare plate, his chair across the table.
Waits for the day when she'll be shown how to grieve, to be inconsolable.

Politics (2)

The Great Highway is eerily quiet. A ring of plovers
dozes by a dune. As if carved from wood,
gray gulls rest along the sea wall.
The ocean is a gray-tinged blue like cornflowers.
Crows squabble over scattered junk food,
flapping, slapping their wings, able
to do real damage striking back with their pin-sharp beaks.
A stooped bald Chinese lady scavenges for bottles
and tin cans in her world of rag and bone.
A hurt crow struggles to escape, streaks
of blood dripping off its feathers, likely doomed to die alone.
Today, the Pacific is peaceful, calm as the lake
I'd swim in mornings naked even after early fall
had chilled the water, as a boy might dare do for joy's sake.

Fascism

When I first wrote of Deutschland in the years
of turmoil after the crash, I noticed how
cops, farmers, shopkeepers broke down in tears
at the slightest provocation. It is different now.

Well-scrubbed streets, proudly spotless houses
in villages and cities. Plowed fields. Fall festivals.
Filled markets. Each thrilling rally that rouses
the nation. Pageantry. The flag-draped halls.

Bayreuth is glorious with Furtwängler at the helm.
Beethoven under canny upstart von Karajan
in Berlin. Great music played throughout the realm,
inspiring all souls, the poetry of the true German.

And our food! Sausages, veal richly sauced, pastries
crammed with sweet whipped cream, the wines,
from Rhineland, my god, each sip I take satisfies
more. The well-stocked stores. Factories fine as shrines.

And schoolchildren reciting patriotic poems, windows
flung wide open, singing hymns as they march into
class to learn of the war's victorious heroes,
of Weimar's betrayal, Versailles' calumnies. It's all new.

And the broadcasts our families raptly listen to no
matter the hour when every great man speaks
to denounce the scum from the East and its low,
vile, bestial hordes, flesh stinking of turnips and leeks.

I've heard what foreigners say, what they write in
newspapers, but it's propaganda, outsiders' lies.
It is not wrong for a nation, neither evil nor a sin,
to favor its own kind. Racial pride is a law of the wise.

It is not wicked, our treatment of Jews and gypsies,
sodomites and the genetically ill-fit. A rusty, dull
knife cuts nothing until honed and sharpened. Seize
power from the weak. Praise hatred. Make men hopeful.

The Flying Dutchman

A last great storm might spare his mind, weary of the chaos at sea,
begging for the tempest
to cease, might cleanse his memory
of battles in the North Atlantic, unable to find rest
from drowned birds, shredded flags, dead faces' looming
over him at night, an ocean-tossed,
wind-battered man at home in a safe room
finally, yet otherwise lost
at sea, his only brother
killed or a suicide on the Russian front.
What can a man do to end the horror
of what he has seen? The burning men he hunted
for in the icy water, their torpedoed ship sinking fast,
his buddies dying for the thousand years the Reich was doomed to last.

Kroll Opera House

No films, no photographs survive of her,
all burned in the war
during the bombing of the theater.
She was a star
in war-time Berlin, but gossip,
ill-founded aspersions
devastated her reputation, though with lip-
service paid to her childhood's miseries. Which versions
of her story are believable? Listen
to her recordings. There's nothing immoral or strange
about them. She sings nothing she'd be forbidden
to sing today. She made no attempt to change
the world, yet nothing about her art was evil or callous.
Murderers praise ruined her. Her fame's unintended malice.

Azucena, That Grieving Mother

1.

On a neglected battleground, bent farmers reap wheat. A highway
courses through fields the war was fought on. Darnel
and mustard bloom among scrub hedges. Soldiers yesterday,
today children bathing in summer streams. It was brutal, a hell
here only decades before, the fighting that followed every dawn,
the sun her child believed to be a bird of prey unfolding its wings.
The white-haired old woman has lost her boy, years ago drawn
into battle in Spain, Italy, France, it doesn't matter where. She sings
the same whatever the place since loss has forced her to go mad.
In nightmares, in a bonfire's mounting flames, her son scares her
as she plots to enact her revenge. And so she rages, the love they had,
the bond they shared greater than a covenant intended to deter
her from shedding more blood, obedient to her hatred, the sun dar-
ing her, her child beseeching, crying, Mother!, No!, and she blinded by its glare.

2.

A troubadour wanders, lute in hand, through the night,
a shade barely seen, hard for his lover to hear
at first, his voice melodious, though frightening
like someone whispering dark secrets in her ear
as behind him smoke dirties the sky
from a distant fire, the singer's face,
as he steps closer sighing
her name, soot black
as the kettle his mother cooks with, the boy of mixed race
maybe, maybe a gypsy, either way subject to the rack
or stake if discovered by his enemy
who is named Luna, Moon (the plot is convoluted), hate
never spent if left unfulfilled, caustic, paradigmatic as the fate
of a mother killing her son by mistake, brother brother in the rites of family.

Anzio

Impoverished son of a carboniere, reluctant soldier in the war,
a boy who delights in strutting like an Italian tenor
before young girls or older women, hundreds of miles far
from home, no dedicated warrior,
a bit of a braggart,
always giving his buddies the bum's
rush by not paying what he owes them, his heart
beating fast, faster when the first bomb comes
and explodes and his sergeant's body bursts like a Sicilian melon,
though he can't say, after the long delay,
why the sky erupts like a brute storm breaking over the Mediterranean,
hitting, striking them by surprise as he and his pals are playing
football on the beach while the American
fleet, a many-headed monster rises, its fiery breath scalding the horizon.

Salò

With his matinee idol looks, his well-coiffed hair befitting
authority, a voice like a trumpet–
powerful, commanding, setting
underlings, scum, whole armies scurrying–why should he let
his country decline into peace so long
as its soul needs purifying by further conflict? Disrupt-
ion, chaos is the law of nations, the marching song
soldiers sing, fervent as a hymn. No mere setback can interrupt
his hold on power, make him afraid
of his compatriot's betrayals. Salò remains at the whim
of his passions, subject to his will. Rome stayed
imperial for a thousand years through torture. Pain does not trouble him,
ever mindful of the sun each morning as it lifts higher, ever more majestic
like a dawning state, bloodying the nation with its glory, violent and fascistic.

Milan

La Scala is celebrating its reopening, the stage
packed with musicians, singers, players, all in the finest of hands:
Arturo Toscanini conducting, Tancredi Pasero, bass. It's the first page
of a new democratic era after the war. Who understands
its operas understands Italy, every seat--box,
orchestra, grand tier, balcony--taken, grander
than before hostilities began or after, the theater then blocks
of rubble laid to waste from the bombings of Milan.

The wisest Italians, of course, worship Rossini, Verdi, Puccini,
Boito since the country's history repeats the absurdity
of plots which only music can turn into tragedy. Verdi's
grieving choruses, his sorrowful Te Deum at a time of liberation,
Mosè's prayer, Manon's despair, Mefistofele's bargaining with God's heavenly
choir. Listen. Vineyards are ripening on sunlit hills. Ulysses sails home on blue seas.

The Last Russian

All I need, I tell myself, is enough time spent in silence
to put down my life's story as I've writ-
ten it in my head, like a medium in a seance
deep in spook land, understand? Knock. Speak. That's it.

Yet it's not so simple, is it?, conjuring the plot
I've thought of without ever commit-
ing it to paper. It's unhappily true. I've got
a wastrel's soul and the mind of a hypocrite.

So I pretend I'm an aristocrat living in a sort of hut,
you see, in a birch forest where fierce wolves
threaten me, soldiers pursue me. I am not cut
out to be revolutionary. How little their dogma solves.

Even alone, I'll imagine I attended balls at court, used
to woo countesses and fine proud princesses,
seduced a few handsome officers, too. I abused
my powers, I'd agree, with my mercurial personalities.

I was always the perfect gentleman, courtly, always
polite, even when I saw them beat their wives
or horses or as I watched their servants raise
red flags in protest of their wretched serf's lives.

In my unwritten story, it's Nineteen Five, you see.
Because I'm in dire danger, I must find solace
and succor in faith. I become a monk. Flee
to birch tree woods to contemplate God's grace.

It's a peace that never comes within my reach,
you'll notice. I comfort myself by opening a window
to the winter outside, hoping it might teach
me better how to confront a people's sorrow.

Or explain to me why I've never written a word. Why
I've lived all my life opposing any revolution,
pretending I was the aristocrat I am not. Try-
ing to be historical. The famous last noble Russian.

The Finnish War

Mountains shadow the besieged city,
their peaks charcoal gray, olive drab
trees like an enemy army
seen from far away.

A waning moon climbs no higher
than the sun at dawn
in mid-winter,
his mind numbed by sleep.

Tanks on an ice-covered roadway
drive through woods fast
as trucks. At woods' edge, fires stay
lit from fear of wolves.

A frozen lake glows blue-
white, locks boats
in ice it would be fu-
tile to try to free.

The call of the sea, whether Baltic
or Arctic, is cold
and impassioned as music
he loves, loud and Russian and bold.

Like a birch wood forest no one
dares to stare into,
he fears the sun
white as snow, white as a Finnish fighter.

There is nothing he does not
believe in as he breathes
the acrid, rot-
sweet smell of Siberian spruce.

He believes God is everywhere. Believes
the earth is good, though winter
lasts forever, grieves
for the day he'll be shot as a traitor.

Korea

The sun had been on fire all summer,
then rain fell on rooftops, thunder
rumbled through woods, scatter-
ing crows. A boy meander-
ing down rows of corn
likes getting wet,
untroubled by storms, watches a hawk borne
skyward by wind. He wants never to forget
anything. Fern fronds. Hail
crackling on asphalt. Ripe apples
picked from a tree. Or night, hard and gray as shale.
Moonlight sneaking through a window. Grackles
black as shadows squeaking like a gate. His brother,
killed in the North at the start of the war.

Wolf Child

Wolf child, boyhood spent
with wolves in the silence
of a forest. Twisted, bent
birch tree limbs, leaves to sleep on,
his disappearance
left unlamented, who won
acclaim when the Erlking
chose him for
the prize, ring
to wear like a charm
when come to harm,
he and his brothers—
the demons he tore
apart, braver than all the others.

Liberation

1.

The scent of the sea spices the air, pine
cones and dune grass, the taste
of salt pungent in spring breezes, resin-
ous as the stand of long leafs behind him.

Scarf tossed round his neck, frayed straw hat
on his head, the elderly man slowly climbs
a ladder to attempt to rescue a feral cat
that a dog chased up a tall white cedar.

With his left arm crooked, he grips a rung
while his right stretches high to free it.
When he looks up, it hisses and lunges
at him just as noon like lightning stuns him.

2.

On Patmos, in an ecstatic vision,
Saint John is transported to
paradise, a blazing, cosmic sun
his guide, freed from exile,

spared stormy seas, desolate skies,
his desires and lusts burned
away, John relieved of memory's
imprisonment, liberated by Christ's

sacrifice to dwell in the new
city of massive golden towers,
bejeweled walls, thrones, blue
crystal, jade columns, carnelian

palaces, a heaven like an eastern
potentate's, rich and orderly,
gated and exclusive, eternal,
beautiful, immortal to those

inside its endless gardens, its Lord
the emperor of order, chaos,
wilderness, anarchy abhorred
Rome restored, the New Jerusalem.

3.

His arms badly scratched, he can't hold the cat
any longer. He lets it go on sandy
soil, watches it dash off, its habitat,
its sole home, the neighboring woods.

A warm wind blows through. The sun drifts
lower. Its light, cat-eyed and wise,
he thinks, gleams slyly knowing, lifts
his spirit with a glow like love's almost.

Tomorrow, he might even try to feed
it, thin, scraggly as it is, to save a few
birds from its jaws, but he still bleeds
where the cat clawed him, refusing to be rescued.

IV

Cat Man

After my mother died in a bleak white hospital room,
her face distorted into a fright mask, I
dreamed of her every night for years as I've
dreamed of my father, too, since the day he slipped away
from one sleep to another like a burglar
fleeing through a window into the dark. Dreams,
like ghosts, are forebodings, I suppose,
memory playing its magic
tricks on us. No matter. When I talk
to the dead, they understand what
I ask. Ghosts aren't real, of course
Yet, my cat-
loving friend, tell me, what is death
like for you living with your god Bastet in your feline heaven?

Library

A man is the books he reads, saves
on shelves in some sort of order,
the words, the pages,
the stories he recalls. A library braves
time in a way, the cover,
the binding, the images
in books like old friends gathering
for a reunion, knowing
how much they've changed. I sent
you a book of poems with a letter
in it. Please keep it. I have leant
it often. I'd bestow,
if I could, every book on my shelves
to friends so they'd know who I was, my variable selves.

Old Year's Moon

Over water, last year's moon hides in shredded
clouds reddened
by haze in the air. This morning
marks the end of a century. I remember
how, young, I'd welcome New Years, spring
not far off with its blessings, no catastrophe
lurking around the next corner.
What does it mean just to be
in the world, to live in the moment? The past lives too far away,
though when it returns it can sometimes stay
too long. You were a great beauty
once, in memory
like a gorgeous bird perched in a eucalyptus
singing, preening too high in the tree to catch or possess.

Pareidolia

Sunset is scorched orange, the moon
scarlet after months without
precipitation. Soon, people say, soon
rain will end the drought,
extinguish the fires. Slips of clouds float
through the sky far from shore
torched by twilight, like sails on a boat
that's burning miles from harbor.

I imagine its men lost. I picture their last meal
Bread. Stew to eat.
Beer to drink.
                    And I remember the emptiness
I felt after you left, unable to tell what was real
anymore. I see a street,
a burned-out house. No phone to call, no mailbox, no address.

The Birds

Meadows and fields and barns well-stocked
with cattle and sheep, corn and grain,
days clocked
by sunrise and twilight. Again,
like last year, finches displaying magenta, orange-red,
or golden crowns, chickadees, sparrows,
swallows, cardinals, long-billed crows,
doves, orioles pecking at what plenty has spread
out before them, songful birds resting in bushes or forests
wishing only to be free of fear, happiest
outside gardens. If you long to relish
the day, go with them. Say yes to their music. Be
at peace. A lone towhee might be the emissary
you need to learn of joy. To perch on a branch of its flowering tree.

Ville d'Ys

A beachside vision of a city
under the sea,
a sunken island
off shore,
a people drowned in water
blue as ice in winter
waiting for more
life and
restoration
from surging waves and surf,
rebirth,
like the sun
rising above the horizon
each morning at dawn's command.

Georgics

Broken-winged winds shedding feathery clouds.
Storm bared pin oak, alder, maple, walnut. An open field
farmed for beans drowned, abandoned. How loud
was the thunder that broke summer, the rain that healed
the drought in outbursts of a ruinous sudden
power? Sheep unshorn, ground unplowed, bees
silenced by dust and heat, no giddy children
laughing under a searing sun. Then rain came to seize
their days from sorrow, the passionate insouciance
of two boys unknown to any city, free in the country,
too green for wars or civic debate, who ran to see
how fast they might race, to taste apples that hung
from trees, unripened pears, to hear what birds sing of, young
enough to believe in themselves, to trust in their vows of innocence.

v

Orest

I have seen men kill, entire families slay each other.
I have swum in brutal seas past coastal shelfs bent,
worn, jagged, riptides clashing. I have watched waves smother
sailors dying tangled in beds of kelp. I went
away for a while, fled home as a storm
howled in my ears, buried bodies in a field of flowers.
Nightmares are the form
life takes when it burrows into the dark of caves. A boy cowers
in my arms. A girl flees
from me unable to bear what she sees.
A wolf kills to eat.
A hawk, a shark must destroy to survive.
But men are worse than beasts, raw, incomplete,
no one left at the end still alive.

I remember my mother like waves breaking
on cliffs, like Odysseus crying about
the wife he left behind, abandoning
his peace of mind, lashing out
at her suitors, her handmaids without sorrow,
feeling no pity
for those he had justly felled. Tomorrow,
Delphi, cheating, deceiving me
of what the unquiet dead bestow
on the guilty. In a field of flowers,
redder than blood where I rage below
against their watchful eyes, roars,
like the machinery of wars, the furies,
avengers, killers of men, destroyers of cities.

The Andromache

1. Andromache's Farewell

Three times Achilles dragged my husband
round our sacred city
unbinding it from Apollo
and his protection. Now I understand
why gods' promises are hollow,
lacking all pity.
They want my son, me
to perish. He is a swallow in a hawk's nest,
I a coney in a lair of wolves.
I fear the lasciviousness of Greeks. I detest
them and their wars. My child pulls
at my hair, protesting my tears.
While Troy is burning to the ground, I know he must die:
a fledgling flung from his roost too young to fly.

2. Andromache's Lament

Like a fury, I'd hasten after his soul's
descent. A red
fire glows
over the city's walls and towers. The dead
see more than the reviled
like me, the soon to be killed or exiled.
They watch me moan and cry
because I cannot bear to watch you die,
Astyanax. Whose child is this
I have kidnapped instead, my heart like stone?
In the presence of the rampaging Greeks, let me kiss
him as if he were my own,
my child though no son of Hector,
and I, his murderer, wailing louder than his mother.

3. Andromache in Phthia

Myths. Lies. Those stories composing my legend. My son is dead.
Another son lives unsafely on, Molussus, scion
of Achilles through Neoptolemus, whom rumors have said
is my lover. Why won't I admit it? I watch a stream run
up to the temple's columns, then flee
back to the sea, pearl-pure in its nacreous beauty.
Childless, barren Hermione,
fiancée to my boyfriend, would kill me if she could. No good
ever comes from a royal's jealousy.
The bitch berates me like a high queen secure
in her birthright, blood-
lust pouring from her tear-reddened eyes, cocksure
of her rights and duty as she stands before me, strut-
ing, preening, defaming me, calling me names: 'Barbarian,' 'Whore,' 'Trojan Slut.'

4. Andromache on Helen

Let Helen never sleep soundly, her heart the foulest, most impure,
vulgarest of the Greeks. My husband was the prize
the gods awarded them for their cruelty, their pillaging nature,
their ferocity. My life has become one disguise
after another. Literature
tries me, condemns me for the child who dies
thrown off a wall over and over again in its pages, a boy my own
or another mother's. Or mourns, laments with me. Whole tragedies
have been written about that one scene, though I alone
know the facts of what happened or once thought I did
while I was there, the one true witness. I am no longer sure
of my own history. To bear children is tragic. Any other truth is hidden
from me, as dark as Zeus. Or Helen, passionate Helen, lascivious
and erotic, divinity, a lesser Aphrodite, seductive, doomed, and perfidious.

5. *Andromache Appeals to Thetis*

Now Neoptolemus has been beaten, defeated, too,
abused, murdered. Seducer, rapist, my savior,
which of the three was he? I leave it to the future
to decide. I must bear
his loss alone. Sanctity
is far rarer, more precious than beauty.
Let Thetis appear to me,
Nereid,
demigoddess of the sea.
I must be wed
again, though I have died many times at the brute hands
and lusts of men. By her shrine, near land's
end, I wait for her to rise, more frightening than Hector
gazing at me as I washed his wounds and bloodstained armor.

6. *Andromache in Molossia*

Tragedy is never reasonable. Always circuitous, it twists
and turns, then aims its arrows to shatter
us, like the dark matter
of the universe, irresist-
ible. Picture me, if you can, as an old Trojan matron
wearing a gold embroidered shawl,
costly possessions scattered about me, finest hand woven
tapestries, delicate pottery, gleaming mosaics on every wall
portraying our victories. A pretty image in a way, isn't it?, a fine old age
for Andromache with Helenus who made, Virgil wrote, a new Troy
in Molossia. Yet daily I continue to rage
against my fate, grow no wiser, suffer like an animal, know no joy,
forced to hear in my unwilling ears the monstrous din
of epic wars and the cries of my city's dying children.

Medea

He said he loved me. I gave him all my amorous magic.
That is the heart of my tragedy. He said he would stay
with me. But he abandoned me for him. Made me sick
with jealousy. I begged him, "Don't go. Don't betray
me." But they sailed together to his lover's city. Say
I am too much the man, though I grieve like a sorceress
wearing a black shawl of mourning on her long way back
up mountains to olive groves where the oldest goddesses
dwell among the smell of sweet fruit under black
summer suns. Demeter, I'd say, Hecate, teach me to live
in sorrow, to sing my threnodies passionately as I thrill
to his fingers on my willing, plaintive body. Dreams, give
him to me, lips, hands, prick, calves, all to kiss. He is my tragic
destiny. We called the days our children. The future I desperately kill.

The Flight into Egypt

Herod, the magi, Joseph, Mary,
peaceable shepherds enacted
in tableaux vivant, the baby
Jesus in the manger a loaned
porcelain doll swaddled in linen—
each depicted near the altar
where he plays a soldier in a thin
cotton tunic dyed to mimic armor,
a boy reluctant to take the rôle
of a cruel centurion sent to kill
innocent Hebrew children, the holy
family fleeing into Egypt
as the boy stands tensely, still
as a statue, holding a rawhide whip.

Lazarus Come Back

I must be a frightful sight, bony, thin, eyes popping out
of their sockets, stinking of rotten meat, a bit wormy.
You will want to hear what it is like, what it is about,
lying in a tomb or deep underground in a cemetery
or tossed to the wind with slaves' ashes. But I have sworn
to keep its secrets. It is good to see you all again,
my friends, my family. You swear I have been reborn.
You claim I'll get better, shed the stench and stain.
It isn't so, though my oath makes me stint on details I'd
tell you of, stories so strange you'd think I'd lied.
Don't expect what you imagine. Don't believe what you've read.
Death is a crowded place, its residents having to shove
and push for space to sleep. Yet I confess two truths about the dead.
They know how not to hope for things. They know too dearly how to love.

Lazarus Saying Goodbye

Alive, I took pleasure in figs, jugs of mellow wine.
I've made of my last meal a seder of sorts, a time
for recall. Life is a feast to be enjoyed, a fine
thing to have after all, even the stain and the grime
of it, but the wars go on and the endless dying.
Revived, I was neither living nor dead, a refugee
of a kind between my two countries, belonging
to neither. I've lost my taste for honey, roast lamb,
dates, feed on desolation since each day I see
how much you are like me, my dear friends, my family,
how much my pain taints your bodies already. I am
afraid to leave again. Out of earth's tumult, I stand on
the shore of the Galilee, wind my shroud back on, son
of no one. If to live is to love, we die by forgetting it. Goodbye.

On the Morning of Christ's Nativity

When Christ was born, Milton wrote, the old gods fled,
the oracles were silenced, the classical temples closed.
But the reign of His compassion never followed, was dead
before it started, the future not what the poet supposed
it might be. It is a rainy, frigid Christmas morning in San
Francisco. The poor huddle in door ways, hospital
corridors, make-shift shelters. There's a countrywide ban
on refugees. Corruption, indecency rule. To suffer is pitiable,
but what can one do when powerless? Another rampaging beast,
its hour come round at last,
is ravaging court and church and state.
The hungry lap at technology's feast
like famished dogs that fast
on what pittance it feeds them. What monsters men create.

My Parents in Eleusis

1.

The sun is submerged in dark, in the sea
or a cavern deep in the earth. Let it be
saved from a world without day or season,
from black-out as if a war is on, wife,
husband, son, daughter raped, all gone.

This is you, left, at the end of your life.

This is Demeter's heart, her child lost, a cave
in the earth where a flame is lit to save
whoever mourns from so much grief.

                A sheaf of wheat shown,
barley, a bowl of pomegranate
seeds are all or nearly all that is known
of the rituals, kept undesecrat-
ed, secret by Eleusis, the truths of its sacred way.

2.

My parents walked it on a blazing hot day
in June when the Colonels ruled the state,
despots, tyrants, jailing opponents
on barren islands, men, women late
of Athens or Naxos or Rhodes, their dissents,
bare humanity denied them.

                My father found
scattered over untended ground
marble rocks and pebbles, like debris from
a nearby gravel quarry. He picked
two up from beneath a broken column
of a ruined temple, gently kicked

the earth to dislodge a third and pocketed
all three, recalling how I had said

the best gift he could bring me back
from Greece would be dirt from the rite's
soil, a relic of its earth.

3.

                    In letters black-
er than jet ink he had had inscribed the site's
name on a clear paper weight–Telesterion
of Demeter Eleusis–had it made for his son
in his company's shop, the three small rocks
secured forever on it by a glue
so strong they could never break off, in a box
he had wrapped for me on holiday from my college.

4.

                    I have a view
of the Pacific from my bedroom, watch the horizon
reunited each night with the sea. The sun's
been abducted further down than a cave,
deeper than earth. Yet at dawn a priest
will rekindle its fire in a rite that will save
it from the dark for another day, releas-
ed once more from Hades.

                    I could say that in many
less fancy ways or just note what is easy
to see. It is long past ghosts-at-midnight
time and dawn will come in a few
more hours. Reigniting doused light
is what religions mean to do.

But why try to paraphrase dawn? I lost
you twice. I waited in the dark, tossed
out of the bar for drunkenness,
too much wine, too much riot on the dance

floor. So I made up a lie out of distress,
said I saw you go with no look back, no backward
glance.

5.

My dad's paperweight is old. One pebble
has broken off the plastic, a stony rebel.
Poetry is animism. I hold in my hand
a chipped rock I am devoted to, a worn icon
I fondle like a worry bead, the land
my fantasies inhabit as I rub it, the one

I would have been born in if I could have chosen it.
My duty, my pleasure each day are to sit
in the gymnasium, waiting my turn,
while watching Kritias, Lysandros wrestle.
Or I stand in the master's grove, learn-
ing pouring from him like wine from the vessel
wisdom is. Here, the ripest olive trees
shine in the sun with a light that pleases
me like the glow off boys' oiled bodies.

Eleusis' is the next holiday, its rites,
its processions, music, dances, thyme's bees'
honey to eat, roses, anemones, flights
of finches, waxwings mine to enjoy.

6.

                    Talismans
or pebbles. I roll one in my hand. Trans-
cendence. The magic of anything
the past seems to cling to, dwell in,
like the spirit of a god in a rock or a ring
transfiguring the ordinary, a pen, a pin,
returning Persephone to her mother, her
my father's shards belonged to, Demeter.

No believer, he stole them for love of me,
stones meaningless to him, three ancient
chips from a temple, not rubble, a plea,

unspoken, to love him back, the discontent
he knew when I stayed cold, unchanged,
as if I'd been abducted, estranged,
taken to some nether world, hidden,
me the child, the son he had had or meant
to have fathered a denizen of the dark, forbidden,
unable to be reborn in corn's, in flame's ascent.

7.

My father and my mother are slowly walk-
ing on a hot June day, sunglasses on, talk-
ing in whispers, late middle aged, almost
old, the mouth to the cave not far
away from where they pause, their host
for the tour pointing to the place. A car

backfires on the roadway. Then all is silent,
wind, trees, birds, workmen. The sun's descent
is as quick as after prey a falcon
flies, wings spread out, beak down. So my father
describes it, the light on the horizon
vanishing like a hawk. Yet the dark doesn't bother
him, nor the stillness.

                    Far away, a flame
flickers—probably, if anything is to explain
it, a light in a window in the distance.
The three stones are safe in his pocket.
He says to his wife he wants to dance
and they do despite the ruins' quiet.

8.

My parents are long in their graves now,
or rather their ashes in urns are on show
in the underworld where they have been
buried. Eleusis is a myth, part history,
part legend. Wheat sheaves, a fire seen
in the dark. Resurrection. Immortality.

And I, who know nothing about either,
fondle a pebble, child of Demeter,
praying it might be so, the magic
that is bestowed on matter, the body
reborn, transfigured, made new, transfix-
ed by desire, by a light I have yet to see.

Palinode (1)

For a moment, I believed that the antique-looking, encrusted cast iron frying pan
I cook with every night was still the one my grandmother had used
like her grandmother before her, belonging to a world older than
I could ever know, until my husband corrected me. He had bought it. I refused

at first to admit it had been his gift only two decades ago. But it is true.
My grandmother's cookware hides in the cluttered back of a cabinet
in our kitchen packed with things I have forgotten, could not enumerate
if forced to. How much of any memory is desire wrongly pursued, beset

by confusion and mistakes? I have too much to learn with little time left me.
Like everyone, I wait for rain, fearing wildfires and a future of untold diseases.
I search for an order that is profounder, wiser than ours, for art and poetry
and music to be meaningful as they were once. I pray for release, for what pleases

gods I never have known, yet regret I'd denied. I beg the Dharma Wheel
to revolve, to turn once more, for Jesus to return. I want some score or poem
to save me, though I'm sure none ever will. I long for a life devoted to real
things, not words alone. I need to learn to say goodbye. To find another home.

Palinode (2)

Nothing living–whether wild or tame, enchained or free,
well-fed or hungry, safely settled in country, in towns or cities,
or dangerously wandering, journeying over land, by air or sea–
nothing, no one is spared mortality's
fate despite what histories preserve, what monuments
display, even poetry no more than a passing reminder
of what once was here, a sign of what the human spirit invents
that for a while helps us to remember
the past like conjurers of spells, like magicians
evoking a lost vision or a longed for story:
like that morning when the sea's breezes where I lived were as saltily
sweet as the incense of smoldering rose wood and glory,
I saw, was the sky opening to the sun as a meadow of black-eyed susans
and Wood's blue asters unfurled to its light while a bird soared over a tree.

Book Two

In Place

Table of Contents

III.

IV.

I

Barrier Island

On the island I used to visit, there are fewer children
now. Tourists come in the summer to pick berries,
explore graveyards where lie those who died long before
we were born. No one is troubled. No one hurries.
Many dawdle, enjoying the inscriptions, the wrought iron door,
gnarled oaks, Spanish moss, crumbling brick walls.
A few ride bikes in the island's small park, greenest when
rain pours in from the sea every day and falls and falls.
The sole ferry arrives from the mainland at dawn,
returns at sunset. It's peaceful after they've gone, once night
has come. The island seems happy. Men play cards, children yawn,
women gossip, darning well worn clothes. So I might rewrite
the past, revise the history of any place whose discontent people, set
in their ways, claim they have no reason to change, nothing to regret.

The Myth of the Cave

Our goal, let's agree, to open to the sky again,
hope worn thin from our ill use,
torn into bits and pieces, the stain
in us difficult to clean after so much abuse.

I despise hiding like an outlaw in a cove
tides flood each day from a rising sea.

I want to see the stars shine above
us and to feel peace at last, to be
rescued from a cave where our shadows
flicker off of candles. I want to look into
your eyes. I want to walk upright, outward
to sunlight, splash like a child in shallows
warmed by summer. I want to gaze up toward
heaven and see it is the day you promised me breaking through.

Progress

We were told history is our destiny. Those who
could leave fled at night on
trains or buses or by foot. Few
risked saying goodbye. It was time for them to run
fast as they could, the age of unreason
descending upon us, of an endless winter
in a perpetual dark
when the mark
of a red flower
inscribed on their faces shames the heathen and alien.

And afterward, after the disease
has ceased, I confess
it now, the state will seize
you who resisted its insistence on progress.

Narayama

It is the last day of his life in the seasonless world
of his dying, cold one moment, the next
burning up. He feels he is being purged
of time, its perplexing
sequences, returning to Eden before the fall,
unable to distinguish one life from another
as in the story of the Valley
of the Seven Turns. His is the winter
snow on Mount Narayama, the hour
when fat crows devour
his liver. Strapped in a chair, he
grasps his carrier's strong shoulders,
refusing to glance back or strain to see
the mountain peak where the wind is blowing
harder. He knows where he is going.
Through woods, up steep rocky trails to wait for birds among black boulders.

Pacification

Rushing ashore before sunrise, the army went
unresisted. Around camp fires, they
sang freedom songs or were content
to make the people sing them, conveying
their joy in liberation, their hundred
words for pain banished from the stories,
about soldiers. In those dreadful
days, silenced, I fled,
intending to tell strangers about my country's
sufferings, how lies became
normal, natural even, a part of the landscape,
as if loss could be made beautiful with a new name,
like the ones they gave to the children set out daily to die,
floating off in little boats, even the bravest too scared not to cry.

Exodus

Come away. In this part of the world, in a time
of drought, dawn comes quickly. Look westward
as hills capture the first rays of the sun. Climb
there, where light arcs earthward.
Mothers, fathers, love
your children. Care for them. Laugh or cry
with them. Gather them in your arms. Move
beyond the river to the further shore. Lie
for a while beneath the warmth of morning. Rest
in a place so unlike your home. An old woman
sits on a stone holding a basket, all she owns, peering
across the plain, past the miles they must trek yet, blessed
she might tell you, to get her first glimpse of a heaven
so unlike the glorious stories she once read that had led her here.

The Green Knight

Flood waters rise where an old knight stands lakeside,
a good man saddened because his country has fallen
prey to blight and decay. Bereft of companions, allied
to no king, he has been strangely taken
by a love for the dark. By night he will have disappeared
into the forest, his quest
ending in woods he has long feared
being summoned to for his life's final test.

Passing hunters poke at his body with their rifles' barrels,
foul as carrion, worthy of their disgust and do not
notify the cops. Why bother? More arduous travels
through wilderness where rot
and decay are common await them. Who would they not let live
for a bit of wine and bread along the way? Who wouldn't they forgive?

Troy

The shaman were wrong, the storms more savage
than they foretold, the wars reducing
their great city to ruins. In another age,
among different people, their old king
dead too, a few fled westward, first to Carthage,
then Rome, but no Troy reborn changes anything.

Through the ages, the rage
and wrath of men remain the same. So sing
of places if you believe a city
is possessed by meanings mythic and perilous.

Sing of a boy's boasting as he hangs his jock in a locker
after a game or another bragging of their victory
or a third, with spit and a curse,
defying the wind that blows off their besieged and stinking river.

St. Petersburg

Hiding on the other side of the square, a man
(he knows himself a coward) watches friends
storm the Winter Palace unarmed. What can
they do, outgunned? It all ends
badly, the Czar's forces at the barricades
shooting as rebels leap up steep marble steps.
At court, they decree arrests, torture, raids—
violence and death the state's only precepts.
Or subtle plots. Drinking river water. Dying of cholera.
Monks decrying heretics. Then the predictable fall, pan-
ic, chaos, revolutionary rage at the bourgeoisie.
Dictatorship. Terror. State killings. A five year plan,
followed by famines. What a lectionary is each age
of Russian history when read stage after inevitable stage.

The Country of Lost Hopes

Stern black-clad women close cracked shutters
against night's storms. Pelicans and terns
flock to the mainland as the island's waters
flood. No one asks why. No one heeds or learns
anything. Homeless men shelter in alleys
while partygoers play games whose rules
no one follows. No one recalls the ways
of the elders who taught them in schools
before the plague. Officials consult experts no one
trusts. They claim the water is safe
to drink, though bread is hard as stone.
No one can recall the names of the gods who forgave
them once. There is no transport left to take them toward
safety. They lie awake in their beds enraged at fate and bored.

A New Country

Strangeness is all he has left to write with.
The strangeness of a creature that gnaws roots
or like a harpy hisses in its
scrawny tree, its breath
bitter as the bitterest fruits.
The strangeness of a man who submits
to the grotesque, who, seeing strange
stains streaking the handsomest
faces, embraces every misfortune. A heart
breaks and dies from words distorted, the plangency
of what stays falsely written. The last strand
of truth has strangeness twisted in it. An art
that waits impatiently to be made knowing nothing ahead
will render it impossible, that no one cares what it should have said.

Normandy

Wild whitecaps crash
on the beach. Sunrise
bleak as deep winter.
Stone pinnacles, a rare
slab cracked by a boulder
and the sea's lashing
panic. A crabber dares
to sail out or tries
to, driven back to shore.
By noon, all is calm again.
No more tears. No more
dawn drama. A quiet, plain
day, rage tamed, the stories
after of soldiers strolling the quai.

Nolichucky River

He lives in a place the smarter young
fled years ago, his home a stark
shack near an unweeded park
used as a campground by strung-
out addicts with nowhere but down
to go, like him doomed to stay
as the old are in a destitute town
that reminds them of their own decay.

Oh jump in the river my boy my boy oh jump in the river and drown.

He draws drapes closed, locks doors.
A new storm threatens. The Nolichucky
rises, rushes through steep gorges.
Black clouds mass. Death scourges
and purifies. He doesn't want to be
anymore. The rain, as he leaps, pours.

Oh jump in the river my boy my boy oh jump in the river and drown.

Gordonsville, Tennessee

Brooms, mops, display shelves, refrigerator dollies,
the warehouse's light fixtures, ladders,
bins filled with nails, screws, uncut keys,
sheet rock–all diving, plunging. Beams crash, paint splatters,
plaster crumbles onto the floor. A stack of bricks topples.
A drunkard stumbles backward. Afterward,
he swears he didn't feel a thing, please
believe him, no pain, hurts, aching however hard
he fell as the tornado hit while he stood in the doorway
watching everything plummeting, falling,
collapsing, flying through the room as he struggled to pray
but couldn't, too frightened to think of the right word
to say, too terrified by the boom of thunder he heard
in the whirlwind, the voice of the Lord roaring the world back to nothing.

Affinity, West Virginia

What befalls beasts befalls men.
A blank bedroom wall,
sheets sleet gray. An open
window, drapes blowing. Skeletal
thighs, pecs, arms. Friends
all gone before him. No heaven ahead.
If a man transcends
himself, what then? His dad bled
to death, his body
cold when he kissed
him goodbye. Who has missed
him but his son? It's been a wintry
summer. One wonder won't leave his head.
His father died unsurprised by angels near his bed.

Eden

Streets bustling with people, dance halls, theaters, bars
open, friends, neighbors meeting freely in parks to talk
or enjoy a picnic together, workers on their way to jobs
on buses, in the subway, museums crowded, packed concerts.

Hikers trekking mountains, clouds misting distant peaks, stars
shining on farmland, swimmers in a river, a long, slow walk
through a forest, horned puffins flying over an island, the throb-
bing pulse of ruffed grouses' drumming, cactus wrens in deserts.

Say nothing in a life could refuse us peace. Pretend nothing harms
us, that it is good that a savior chose to pay a high price
for our sins, for Buddha to pray for release from self. Yet, if no trace
of us remains on earth after death, can we say life has graced us?

Imagine the good of creation had caught the world in its loving arms
before it fell from god's favor. Would we still say of paradise,
however hazily or poorly recalled, it was the solitary, walled-off place
where, for our salvation, we came to believe we had been happy once?

II

Testimony

Hedgerow and witch hazel, thickets of wild
ivy silhouetted on snow. Twilight's
looming shadows as darkness thickens. A child
tugs his kite's
string hard, grasps
it tighter until it stings so badly he lets it fly,
watches while tiny as a dust speck it passes
out of sight into a blackening sky.

He lies on fresh snow, loamy rich earth
below it, makes angel's wings
with his arms. The moon is giving birth
to an evening glow, the rings
around it gold and blue
like the sheets of ice it shines through.

Miracle

Blank spaces are for the images that fail,
where the living lie beside the dead
buried under stones. Read the tale
of Jairus' daughter, led
to the gospel by your need for a miracle.
Try to understand, try to listen
better, unbearable,
as the death of a child is. Envision
yourself like her playing beside
her brothers near a well. When a man appears
in the midst of the crowd, she runs to hide,
fearing the death he bears
within him if he dares to touch her,
unaware he has come to save her, Jairus' daughter.

Shipwreck

Cast off, out of sight,
ship's shorn sails, gulls' cries,
bones brittle as shells, a night
you spend in fear, the lies
told about you mounting
like waves, swirling like whirlpools,
you in the sea of them, drowning in ridicule.

The dread of mockery arrives swiftly
each night after
you've fallen asleep, dreamer,
no survivor
of catastrophe,
shipwrecked, the ocean you flail in cold as its laughter.

Victoriana

Old photos' morbidity.
A ship wrecked at sea
on the beach reeking
of tar and gunpowder, curiosity
enticing folks to the dunes
to see it. A man hanged
who had plundered
houses, the crowd, balloons
for heads, cartoons
in a way, gawking, happy
to be part of the scene,
many smartly dressed,
pointing at the body, keen
for death, out for a lark.

Nocturnal

Dark dark dark. The sky, the waiting hills,
earth inviting night into windows,
through mirrors. The dark that fills
the streams, the bay, the rows
of poplars by the park. What is it saying?
Deep into evening, the sky is noon-
time in its spirit. Moon lit clouds sing
in harmony with sleepers, in unison
with enclosed things. Forgive my sins
each time the night begins
anew, confounding far
with near. Dark is the nothing we are,
night spilling over us like a river
flooding its banks in the aftermath of winter.

Portents

A guy on a skateboard
crashing on a crack
in the sidewalk. A hoarder,
black plastic sack
slung over his shoulder
grubbing from a trash can.
Graffiti scrawled on a sea
wall. Two women tattling
to each other secrets
about their lovers. A bull-
dog licking the scab-dirty
face of a grizzled old man
snoring in a doorway. A full
moon. A scrawny black cat. Night sweats.

Tag

Children are playing tag as the sun
descends behind Bearfoot Mountain,
girls and boys running
free in the fields after the rain
while an old man watches
them having fun
though he itches
to join them as he would have done
when young, straying
into woods
where he loved
to hide among his childhood's
friends, changelings who lived in
underbrush or nestled in trees, wild, nobody's kin.

Teddy Bears Picnic

Saturday mornings, lingering in bed,
covers erected with pillow pegs into
a pup tent, five teddy bears
keeping me warm, two
missing a button each wears
for an eye, the day ahead
a surprise we'll discover in the forest,
my stuffed friends and I,
a picnic like a holiday feast, spread
out on a table deep
in woods, trees, sky, a creek, the best
of times before me, like waking from sleep,
a reality no less
real because I find it alone in my wilderness.

Starlings

In a grove burned last fall,
eight pine trees charred
like beams for a wall
of a building marred,
marked, ravaged,
cinders, ash scattered
on ground where years ahead
little will grow, wasted, gutted.

Below a dark oak lightning
struck, starlings preen
on debris, white-
spotted black birds shining
in the sun like the flight
of birds brushed in ink on a Chinese screen.

An Island Story

I could not foresee how long I'd endure
the fantasy
I conjured to ensure
I'd be the one to survive. In a movie,
zombie-thin men beat
drums for those who can neither die
nor live. I greet
you on their island like a shaman.
Around us, naked men
blow conch shells noisily,
loud as they can. With a sharp pen
knife, you carve my face in wood,
toss it to the sea where I die as I should
in a rite of passion, primitive and without mercy.

Anthology

The book I am reading erects a wall
between me and the world, its words
protecting me from harm,
guarded by its bindings, safe in all
its pages. But birds
gliding past my window alarm
me with their ominous signs. Storied
masters, you wrote
in your poems how words glorified
the earth. But I note,
despite your inquisitive eyes,
how all the world says otherwise
and refuses to be, call
it nature's pride, unlike you, anthologized.

Blizzard

Walking from Carnegie Hall into a fierce blizzard,
I miss my bus's last stop, try near Fifty Fifth
to catch another, walk down slick stairs toward
the subway, board it though its crowded with
Christmas shoppers, discover its going south
not north too late, escape, outside the entrance
take a right, each breath like ice in my mouth,
my face freezing, pass a bar with dance
music playing, a truck's tires whining as they grind
in the slush, streetlights buzzing, a bitter wind
wailing past a row of tenements, through high wires,
radio static seeping out a bizarrely open transom,
the singer's voice distorted to the noise of crackling fires
as I listen, succumbing to the snow, to being nowhere home.

Civilization

1.

A warm May morning. A jogger waves as he runs
past, flags flapping from a brownstone, bright
with rainbow colors. A taxi, flashy pink and white,
dashes through traffic, zigzagging lanes. The sun's
being squeezed between two high rises. Waiting
for the light to change to cross into the park,
I hear, near dock's edge, a tug's horn baying
like a sick dog. In a corner playground, darkened
by shadows from a looming brick building,
children rock on teeter-tooters, young men shoot
baskets, a grown woman twists chains on her swing,
giddy with laughter as she twirls. Tonight, The Magic Flute
plays at the Met, an opera so humane in its happy
sad music it glows, radiant as this city in spring, noble and ordinary.

2.

I walk from a dance recital at the City Center into a blizzard,
misread where the bus stops on Forty Third Street,
and descend into the subway instead, though it's hard
to know which train I should take. The snow's turned to sleet
when I emerge from under ground into the Village,
Washington Square packed with people frolicking
in the storm, having fun despite the cold, whatever age
they are. Christmas grows near. A cop car is whining
far away. A slightly sloshed drag queen skids
on ice. Dimmed streetlights blink and sputter, wind
sighs down through a corridor of brownstones. Kids
salute each other on their way home. Sweet music seeps
through open shutters, Schubert I think. One weeps
for joy sometimes without reason. How good this world can be. How kind.

III

Abstract Expressionism

For days, I wander through each massive room
showing The New American Painting, pictures
ornate as Medieval tapestries, superb as the tomb
of Perneb at the Met. Only my elation assures
me of the truth, the reality of what I am seeing.
The galleries are nearly empty. Before an immense
Rothko, an old lady grabs me, says she sees nothing.
 "Why do you look so dazzled?" she asks. "They're nonsense."

Sixty years tardy, I relate this story: sleepless
one night on a camping trip near Ravens Lake,
waves lapping, a white mist steaming off water,
I saw a man in a canoe with net and pole, I confess
I might have been dreaming, intent on catching from the wake
of the moon some rays of its light, as a poet might do or a painter.

Hoopla

My world is her Weimar, as fast falling apart. Lenya
clutches a shawl wrapped round her shoulders,
eager to smother her lover in it. An act. Hoopla.
She taps her foot, her mouth turned down, savors
the banjo being played sour as the twenties
in Berlin, despair, bread lines, riots, trillion mark
notes. But there is a freighter, Pirate Jenny's,
she tells me, waiting in the harbor for us to embark.

And a ship with skulls for masthead, five sails, and fifty
cannons carries me and her away to a life below
the equator where I, maddened by tropic fog
and a fever blazing from a sun that is always angry,
rage at you. Take that pipe out of your mouth, you dog.
Politics makes us bitter, Johnny. Save us from this place. I love you so.

Elisabeth Schwarzkopf

1.

Please don't ask to see me. My looks have aged badly.
Listen to my recordings, I beg you. Try to hear
what beauty meant to me. Severity
is part of art. I am my harshest listener.
I believe in the past, what one hears
in my many records, despite the aspersions
made against me, mannered, arch, the years
when I am said to have behaved badly,
young and desperately poor. Conversions
are rarely trusted. I admit my ambition. Listen,
when I sing, don't you feel a lost world being
restored, a world abandoned, forgotten,
heartbreakingly lost? You're going home where
you'll feel no less sad yet more real somehow. To dare
to be more than yourself is the heart of artistry.
Where are the years? On stage, I enacted many a countess,
giving to each my voice, the nostalgia in it, the troubled largesse.

2.

I am listening, incessantly over and over,
uncannily I admit, while writing this poem
to Elisabeth Schwarzkopf singing
Marietta's lied from Die Tote Stadt.
Ages ago, she told an Austrian writer
that nostalgia, the longing for a home
one's lost, could be heard in everything,
every note she sang. I wonder if that
is why I find myself frequently in tears
hearing her voice, as if it is regret
for past things that brings the lost years
back, like someone you can't forget
having loved so deeply he appears long
after his death, no ghost, incarnate in a song.

Ross Marbury

Decades after the last plague devastated the city, I still
see Ross waving, crossing the street at Castro
and Nineteenth, greeting me walking down the hill
to meet him, shouting, "As I live and breathe," blow-
ing me kisses, repeating "As I live and breathe, you are a sight
for sore eyes," his Alabama accent thickened
by heaven's Southern angels. Sleepless, late at night,
I know no loss can ever be ended
if I keep sighting dead friends jogging in the park, getting
up from bed groggy in the early morning, resting beside
me in the dark while we watch a movie, standing in a restaurant
waiting for a table whenever I pass by. I want them to be alive. I want
them never to have been sickened. I can't keep from hoping
in my folly that we and the great world inside us might never have died.

Kathleen Ferrier

A voice is the soul embodied.
Sometimes I sense as I sing
the presence of the dead in me, pleading
to return to us, to bring
us their gifts, the old
masters, Bach, Purcell, Handel. Their past
is the memory of who we were retold
in art. My body cannot last
much longer. My illness
foreshadows what I will mean to others some day. I feel weighed
down, the shock of my bones splintering inside me.
I am often cold from fevers. If I were to confess
my faith, it would be this: music is the greatest mystery
of life, more sacred than a church or shrine. Why should we be afraid?

Old Poet

For weeks, I could detect the smell
of him on his letters. Fans came
from all over the country, stayed to tell
strangers of their admiration. Fame
is often a mistake. He never began his final
manuscript. When I dream of him
I always see him writing away, banal
I know, my trust in dreams, the slim
chance of any ever proving to be true.
But in the pale light of early
morning, just yesterday, there he
was in a packed room just as I knew
him best, wearing his bright white linen
suit reading poems he had left unwritten.

Peter Pears

Ben insisted he could hear my voice
in all the music he wrote,
its ethereality, I suppose, like a boy's
treble, each note
disincarnate, purer
than a man's more passionate
sound, silvery moonlight on water,
precise and clean. A singer's timbre is his fate.
Lately, I've been wondering if I am a child
who died too young
to have known a grown-up love. Boys' voices beguiled
Ben, happy to wander among
cherubim cast out of heaven
for no reason save the beauty they had been given.

The Lost Boys

An enraged neighbor has scrawled in chalk
on the plague-closed Great Highway,
"Surfers, stay home. Go away."
Warily, my dog and I walk
past five jogging to the beach,
young, strong, and invincible.
No one ancient as I could teach
them anything. "I never get ill,"
one argued yesterday, the sea,
riding the waves purifying
him, the thrill of that freedom
more intoxicating than getting high.
Which is what Barrie called Neverland: land of the young
and eternally heartless. The forever lost boys the old live among.

Janet Baker

During the war, I'd stroll with my father holding
my hand through the moorlands,
desolate and lovely as listening
to Brahms' Rhapsody. The world expands
to far off places where so few trees grow.
In a scrub thicket, by a covey of quail,
I spotted a young rabbit, head severed by a blow
of a poacher's trap. My father went pale.
I turned my head away.
We were all hungry
then, especially workers in the pits close by.
When a memory
like that returns, I think I know why.
I cannot sing without feeling the pity
of living, every song I sing like I'm bidding goodbye.

Rewritten

1.

Brunetto Latini persuades Dante
not to damn him to hell. Othello
exposes the lies of Iago, drowned at sea
as he flees Venice. Ishmael fears go-
ing whaling on the Pequod, dockside
sketches it sailing away. Quentin Compson,
Shreve McCannon, newly lovers, hide
among bohemians in Manhattan.
Meursault's Arab friends save him. Benny
Profane, therapist, treats paranoiacs. Godot
greets Gogo and Didi by a flowering tree,
apologizes profusely for being such a slow
poke. Jake fucks Lady Brett. Marguerite is gaily fêted
at eighty-two. Hamlet kisses Ophelia who's blissful he'd waited.

2.

I would rewrite the world if I
could to satisfy my wish for
happy endings, to magnify
the chances for the right order
of things to get restored
to where they ought to be.
You might object you'd be bored
by lives relieved of tragedy,
by knowing before it starts how
the story will resolve in the end.
But what if you took your bow
before great applause, sending
the audience home glad to see
what should end sadly become a comedy?

Dietrich Fischer-Dieskau

Wild storms long tortured the Dutchman. I am weary of the sea,
too, a mariner of a sort, exhorting the tempest
to end, tired of torment, the Russian front, my memory
of battle. Wagner believed he might find rest
in love. Senta weaves at her loom
while she sings of an ocean-tossed,
wind-battered man suddenly appearing in her room
after centuries doomed to wander, lost.
When does any nightmare end, a better world begin?
My brother was murdered by Nazis who destroyed
our home while I fought for my country. Its sin
is mine, deployed
by a nation that hides its guilt behind its artists. Wars
leave wounds that never heal. I committed crimes. Art reveals my scars.

Revisions

Four decades ago, I wrote a story
about a soldier returning home
to a poor tobacco farm—poverty
all he'd seen, all he'd known
in life—to his family's clapboard
shack trashed by scum who'd used
it to booze or screw in, who'd scored,
scrawled girls' names, words he refused
to repeat over bare walls. Butts
littering floors, glasses and dishes
broken for fun, jackknife cuts
slashing shades and bed cushions.
While he'd fought on Saipan, his father died,
his mother soon after, his brother in France a suicide.

Their four photos lined a mantel, framed
under glass meanly cracked, the brothers'
eyes blinded with ink, both shamed
with obscenities in lipstick, smears
of red crayon on jeans. Instead of fleeing,
he torched the house, watched
it burn as if flames could purify
the earth, observing it as detached,
numbed as he'd been on Saipan, incapable
of grieving, bodies severed, torn apart
by artillery, blackened by flame throwers.
I titled my story after a gnostic fable
about how the demiurge, like a satanic upstart,
rages on earth a cosmic combat against sublime angelic powers.

But the abandoned shack my friends and I
stumbled on in woods near Snake Lake
looked lived in, we the first to trespass it five
years after the war, careful for the sake
of its people not to disturb it. Its last
calendar was dated forty-two. It was strange

to see deep in a forest lives now past
exposed in photos on a mantel, an arrangement
of paper flowers on a table, cutlery
in drawers, a few hefty books–dusty,
well thumbed–open on a homemade
shelf, pillows plumped on beds, ready
for weary heads to rest on. I was eight, confused, said
to be a bright boy, though ill adept at separating the real from the uncanny.

Which is why, grown-up, I had my soldier
discover his home desecrated when he came
back from war. It is easier to condemn horror
to the flames, to deny reality, to blame
the creator for man's self-created evil
and history's disasters, the body's lusts
for the suffering and disgust that fill
most tragic stories of remorse than to trust
the images of what we have left behind
us after our deaths to protest the abandonment
of all we have been. What do I now find
to tell by prying into my childhood's past? A dent
in time. I swear, that day we trespassed, I saw the two brothers playing
in the woods until, startled, they ran away, afraid I might say something.

As If Sung Upon the Water: Delius

A drizzling mist is the last of yesterday's rain.
It is early May, yet the air remains biting as winter,
the sun on his face chilly as earlier
in spring when, like a large basin
overflowing, runoff from snow in December
had flooded the pond. The wind sounds sinister
to his ears. Each leaf, sprig, petal, fern drips
to the beat of an insistently ticking
clock. He is trapped in his body, moves
nothing save tongue and lips
to eat, sitting in his chair, listening,
blind, to his garden, waiting for evening to let
him hear the hoopoes, wrens, robins, cuckoos
sing to him of the glories of all that make music by last light of sunset.

Steve Arkin

En route elsewhere, a Muscovy duck
lands stranded in our neighborhood,
misguided, it appears, or out of luck.
It could be starving. It might find food

in nearby lakes, but birds are harassed
there by raccoons and the water's algae-
infested. Solitary, alone, it crashed,
though programmed to be migratory.

Why did it stray? A neighbor's posted
a lawn sign begging passersby
to treat it kindly. Bewildered, lost
in a strange country, unable to fly

with the rest of its flock to Mexico,
it is a beautiful bird with white,
sleekly black feathers, a red so
bright round its beak it shines in flight

like sunset on a plane. I tried to find
it while walking at dawn, some sign
of its survival, proof that kind-
ness endures in things, some divine

purpose like that of Spinoza's Nature
naturing which he insists takes
God out of creation's picture
while freeing the world from His mistakes.

It is a particularly desperate time
to admit while a plague is infesting
so many—like committing a crime
almost—that existence could be a blessing.

A dear good friend is dying. His wife
writes it is Bach, Mozart, Schubert, gospel
he listens to near the end of his life,
to hear the peace music makes possible.

James Holloran

He is searching for his friend
who went before him. Sometimes death
takes others quicker. Until the end
comes, music is breath
to him. He feels a need
for a remote country,
a new breed
of lover to explore valley
and meadow, mountain peak
with, emboldened by cold wind
as in the inn below,
too far away to seek
to return to in the dark, they see, twined
together, arm in arm, living people, spared their sorrow.

Mazurka: Chopin

He dreams, dreams incessantly because his
soul is always Poland, the dance he is dancing
as he lies in bed at night, coughing,
the rains falling far too late, the lost bliss
of clean air to breathe, precious as a forest
in his homeland, as the aristocratic ball-
rooms of a grand era, his lungs sorest
while he composes, beating time, in thrall
to the right melody's evocation of the sight
of a beautiful girl he had loved young lying
beside him deep in woods they had fled to, remote,
past barns, pigsties, wheat fields, running at night
in the days of persecutions, rebels murdered, bleeding
in cells while Poland dances madly to a mazurka he wrote.

Nanos

He knows the gods' ways, mountains' quiet, magic
surviving in stones and trees and birds, tragedies
of the everyday, the ordinary sacred, the thick
light of late dawn soaking the islands and the seas
around them with gold. He's a disheveled man in a worn
black shawl mourning the days
he had lost pretending atheism to the scorn
of his neighbors. Look at him, the coast
below where he washes at a well by the maze
of a temple's toppled posts, pediments, lintels. How lost
he would be without the sun's arousing the smell
of lemons and fennel and resinous leaves. Let him tell
you about it, about the earth he worships, the sensual
heaven and sands his songs would call back. Let his death be that lyrical.

IV

Hoh River Valley

A chill winter mist through trees, the pale
play of early morning light. Moss
dangling from trunks, limbs along a trail
like long grizzled beards crisscrossing,
weaving through the forest.
Big leafed maples, sitka spruce
scary, shaggy as primeval
giants who would dance sun-blessed
by dawn antlered like elk, moose
furry in woods before the universal
cold descended and froze them into
ghostly poses, shedding dew-like tears
unable to pray as often they used to do,
as men would, too, from their oldest fears.

That Which

That which he cuts from oak, a two by six, seven
feet tall, stripped, sanded, edges neatly beveled.
A plank. A life. Nothing more. Again and again,
building a life. A beam or support or column chiseled
to fit where it belongs, nothing bent or crooked
to it, as easy as cutting a big oak down with ax
and saw for the raw material. Just matter. Facts.
A plank like that which simply stands, no hands
needed, upright as it must be, that which withstands
sorrow's assaults as he works in his room, never relaxing,
always busy, that's survival's true secret which
everyone knows. It's the keys they've lost. No use in switching
jobs this late. So says Adam. That which leans, flat,
against a wall, is bound to fall. Like him. Like societies. Like that.

Like That

His family crouches by a fire sucking on pig's thigh bones.
In the dark, their cave bleeds red from embers.
Wolf scat lies scattered on its floor hard as stones.
(Notice how night defines his dream's perimeters.)
His mother combs out knots from her hair, preens
like a bird before she flies away, flapping like a hawk.
His father dances to a fiddler's tune and softly keens
as he roasts more meat he's torn on a spit. Try not to gawk
at the boy who wanders the alleys of the borough
begging for sustenance. Any attempt to wake him fails.
Let him be. Let him try to flee, escape his life below
for the life above if he can. Look how his gaunt face pales
at sunrise. Like a devil child, he smells like hell. Like a straying cat
found flayed in woods, betrayed by its family. Like that like that like that.

That's Him

That's him who's leaping feet first into a lake
off a float, holding his breath, touching
bottom quick as his lungs start to ache,
swirling back up, flailing, ears ringing.
banging his head on a plank of the float,
not drowning, not yet, desperate for sky,
air, the light of day, for a man in a boat
to save him, a boy blacking out, young to die.

That's him, old, staring out a window
at his garden
blooming below
as the moon rises like a shadow
over the man
in the boat who's rowing faster to rescue him again.

That When

It is when he determined nothing could be otherwise
that happiness came, though six decades
late. He wonders why the earth fades
from sight, why approaching the end human eyes
see nothing clearly, not love or all he thought he hated
about living. How quickly time came and went,
not to his surprise of course. Was it fated
or did he choose his loneliness? The few letters sent
him he often left unopened or unread. You must know
the reason. He depended upon
the past too much. How sweet and slow
he felt life could be in the sun-estranged wood
he hoped would prove his refuge. That good
pine forest, its trees redolent of last things. That sanctity. That when of eden.

Dancer

A mole on your shoulder. One hand
gripping the bed board as it creaks.
Strong calves. Sweaty thighs. Sand-
paper calluses. Bristled cheeks.
Balls persimmon sour. Sea salt
on tar-slick hair. Coal black eyebrows.
Onyx irises. Lips like dawn's exaltations.
No pledges, vows, tomorrows.
Our bodies self-shedding, two snakes
sloughing off last year's skins. Stiff
pricks, nipples roused and rosy.
Frenzy, desire, whatever it takes
to turn flesh into dance, like a glyph
to be read, your choreographed carnality.

Today, clouds linger over the bay.
The sea is an antique dull pale
olive green. How now to say
I didn't want it to be over? A snail
lies crushed on the pathway, its shell
amber flecks scattered on white
powdered sand. How to write, tell
you that I loved you? A spot light
falls where you dance while my heart
watches you practice at the barre,
observing yourself in the mirror
for mistakes as you learn your part
in a rôle you are perfect for, an art
so erotic it fades as it is made, unrepeatable.

Threesome

After the bar closed, three in a double bed
exploring in storied woods like children
forbidden to wander off late at night, led
by boys' curiosity to a forest hidden
from them by an unmarked border
between them and wilderness, senses heightened
by their daring, trekking through the blur
of leaves, thickets, ferns to a creek that fed
into a lake, inviting, warmer than day
as they swam side by side or dived down deep
keeping eyes shut while touching bottom,
coming up to breathe, to say
how sweet it felt to swim but now it is time to sleep
on banks made soft by beds of reeds, the night this late dawn lit and calm.

One Night Stand

A shepherd chances on a forgotten, archaic
king's tomb dug into a hillside
of the Peloponnese, the walls thick,
the earth rich with shards and treasures he'll hide
by leaving them where he found them: a golden greave,
scattered pottery, a battered shield embossed with a hero's story.
He'll never return, vows never to try to retrieve
such precious things, his last best chance for wealth and glory.

A diver hired at great expense discovers
a bronze kouros lying in mud at the bottom
of the sea in murky waters
churned by tides, but swears to his patrons it was a phantom
they saw, no more than sun's rays fathoms
deep playing its illusion of moonlight on a temple's marble columns.

Unfaithful

He tries to concentrate on the darkness until
he no longer has to think, the black
silence inside him shrill
as a moment of panic
swelling, his heart beating fast.
His stomach hurts. His body
engorges, hog-sized, vast
as a pregnant sow. Come see
him. Come bear witness to a fool.
His bones shred to splinters. His eyes sting
from sweat. Ridicule
him. His vacancy. His empty fling
with another. Feed him nettles, sticky weed, rue.
What could he say? I don't love you. I don't love you.

Break-up

His train rides slowly on worn-out track
while climbing over a mountain
pass, zig-zagging back
down to a river bend and an open plain
on the first day
of May, scrub trees, wild roses, butterflies
in a glorious meadow a thousand miles
from me, from everybody
he had known before he left to be
someone different in a new world.   What would he say
in a note? "I am leaving
without reason
and never coming back." His train hurtles through Spring
Hill. Clicketyclack over clamorous track, on and on.

Jouissance

Jonquils brighter than the sun, a creek, a red clay
path, ivy, dogwood, a paradise made
for us, afternoon light soft as dawn's, cardinals, a jay,
a feral cat baiting ravens, the jade-
pale green of May grass,
chipmunks, squirrels, their fur brown as pine bark,
a lake, of course, a no trespass
sign askew on the fence, tadpoles, newts, a woodlark
singing in an elm tree, the two of us alone,
school let out early, a late spring storm, on our own,
in the rain stripping out of our wet clothes,
standing naked before each other, no one knows,
no one can believe what it is I feel twenty years later
when I meet you like this, like my fantasy of us ardent for summer.

Good Friday

Drink. This high in the mountains,
far from roads and trails, the water is safe,
creeks and streams filled to overflow by recent rains
and snow melt. Quaff
what you can hold, cold as it is in the cup
of your hands. The birds stay still
as stones. No bushes rustle from creatures
scurrying in the underbrush. It is the willessness
of creation that silences the day, what endures
past understanding. Its impassivity.
Be quiet as it is. The air you breathe is sharp as ice. Look up.
The sky is a dusky white like a temple dome inside,
hard as marble, as empty of images. There is nothing to see,
you see. And the God you believe in has nothing to hide.

Holy Saturday

A lonely old charwoman who works only on weekends
dreads Saturdays. It is her job, mopping floors, that lets
her survive somehow. She has no friends.
As she scrubs down each office, she forgets
the life she leads, reading from out of date newspapers
left open on desks. Hesitantly, fearfully,
she rides from floor to floor on empty elevators
she wipes down hard as she can, to clean the filth sweeping through her city.

A scholarly man waits in his book-laden rooms
for it to come, fearing it might greet him quite
quickly, like a grim statistic. It looms
before him, if his calculations are right,
no matter how he runs the figures. Reason
is his persecutor. Or logic.
The biologically rational ordering of the world soon
to be victorious and he listed among the anonymous in a tally of the sick.

A nurse for over three decades, she's frightened for the fate of
her patients, ill and frail and older,
though a few are young. Sometimes doctors shove
her aside, so rushed they are while she's drinking water
from a bottle, reading a chart, fixing her cap,
or squeezing down the crowded hall. She's exhausted by all of it
on a night without promise, allowing no time for the briefest nap
as she adjusts respirators in rooms where patients' faces appear to be masks ill-lit.

You remember how it was the first Saturday after the crucifixion,
all of us packed together in a small, dark room
afraid for our safety, each feeling alone
in his own way, too frightened to visit his tomb
despite how deeply we mourned him. Yet
there he was, still among us we thought, as if borne back to us
by our grief perhaps or our refusal ever to forget
him or that hope we feared might be more bitter than our loss was and as endless.

Easter Morning

High tide breaks over rocks, tugging shell shards and driftwood
back into sluices and pools, washing the sand
where snowy plovers scurry and feed. The neighborhood
is quiet, not even the surfers out yet. He has nothing planned
for the day, the world still unsafe. The sun is a pale flat
disc over hills, whiter than waves' crests until its thick
light flames yellow, expelling night into shadows. That
is much of what he wants to say. How dawn is like the music
played in rhymes, the surprise of the anticipated gift fully given.
A flock of gulls lifts off the beach as they do time after time,
season after season. The beach is deserted. If this were heaven,
this brilliant light gleaming off their feathers, then let it shine
for no reason. Light often tricks the eye, turns fact into mythology.
If all of life is a holy fantasy, then let it be this, this glimpse of you, this clarity.

Peter Weltner taught English Renaissance poetry and prose and modern and contemporary British, Irish, and American fiction and poetry at San Francisco State for thirty seven years. He has published twenty books or chapbooks of fiction or poetry, most recently *Antiquary, Poems and Stories, Vespers on Point Reyes, Selected Poems 1989-2019, Late Thoughts*, and *In the Half Light*. He lives with his husband in San Francisco by the Pacific.

CPSIA information can be obtained
at www.ICGtesting.com
Printed in the USA
LVHW092237070820
662303LV00010B/1131